Perspectives
Plastic
Helpful or Harmful?

Series Consultant: Linda Hoyt

Flying Start
to Literacy®

Contents

Introduction

Is plastic helpful or harmful?

Plastic is amazing: it is waterproof, it can be moulded into countless shapes and sizes, and it can be used over and over again.

But plastic can be harmful! More and more plastic is ending up as waste in our oceans. This plastic waste injures and kills many sea animals.

So, what can be done? How can you help stop plastic waste?

You can see
the difference . . .

a turtle cannot.

Straw no more

In 2017, Year Four student Molly Steer started the Straw No More project. Molly lives in Cairns, which is a town near the Great Barrier Reef in Australia.

What could you and your friends do to make a difference to the amount of plastic being wasted?

" Plastic straws don't ever go away. The very first plastic straw you ever used is still on this planet. "

Molly Steer

When nine-year-old Molly Steer found out about the problem of plastic waste in the ocean, she decided she had to do something about it.

Molly watched a documentary about rubbish in our oceans and how many animals it kills. "All my life I've loved turtles and turtles are most affected by plastic. They get straws stuck up their nose and swallow plastic bags and die."

Molly wanted to help the animals on the Great Barrier Reef, which is right next to her hometown of Cairns. She asked her school to stop using plastic straws, and it did. She asked other schools to ban plastic straws, and they did, too.

Molly succeeded!

By December 2018, about 700 schools and universities in 14 different countries had taken the Straw No More pledge. Almost 500,000 students and staff were involved.

This is how she did it:

1. Molly made the decision to say no to plastic straws.

2. She told her friends at school what she was doing and why, and they joined in. Molly's teachers joined in, too, and so did the school.

3. Molly and her friends talked to their friends at other schools.

4. Molly was interviewed on television and radio, and in the newspaper. When other schools found out about what she was doing, they joined in too.

5. Schools in the United States, Asia, England and New Zealand started to contact Molly. They wanted to join the project, too.

Molly's advice for living straw free:

- Decide to stop.

- If you need to use a straw, choose a straw made from bamboo, paper or stainless steel.

- When you buy a drink at a shop or café, make sure you say that you don't want a plastic straw. Tell the staff member why.

- Ask the staff members at the café to join the Straw No More project as a way to show their customers they care about our planet.

You can find out more about the Straw No More project at: www.strawnomore.org

Speak out!

Plastic is really useful, but do we need to use so much of it?

Read what these students think about whether we use too much plastic.

Some plastics are okay. When your pet has a scratch on its face, a plastic cone is helpful for protecting it. But things such as plastic bags are a problem. We use lots of them. They end up in drains and then in the ocean.

My dad showed me a photo of a whale that had died. Its stomach was full of plastic. Whales can't tell the difference between plastic and an animal they want to eat. They eat the plastic, and then they're not hungry. They don't get real food, and they die.

At home, we stopped using shower gel because we found out that it has tiny bits of plastic called microbeads in it. These go down the drain and into the ocean. Fish eat them and then we eat the fish. This means that we are eating plastic.

Lots of food comes in one big plastic packet, which has lots of individually wrapped items. That's lots of useless wrappers and plastic. If we start getting rid of this useless packaging, we could save the earth.

Is all plastic bad?

Mark Lewis is a deep-sea diver. He is also an ocean scientist. He has a message about plastics.

Why is this message important?

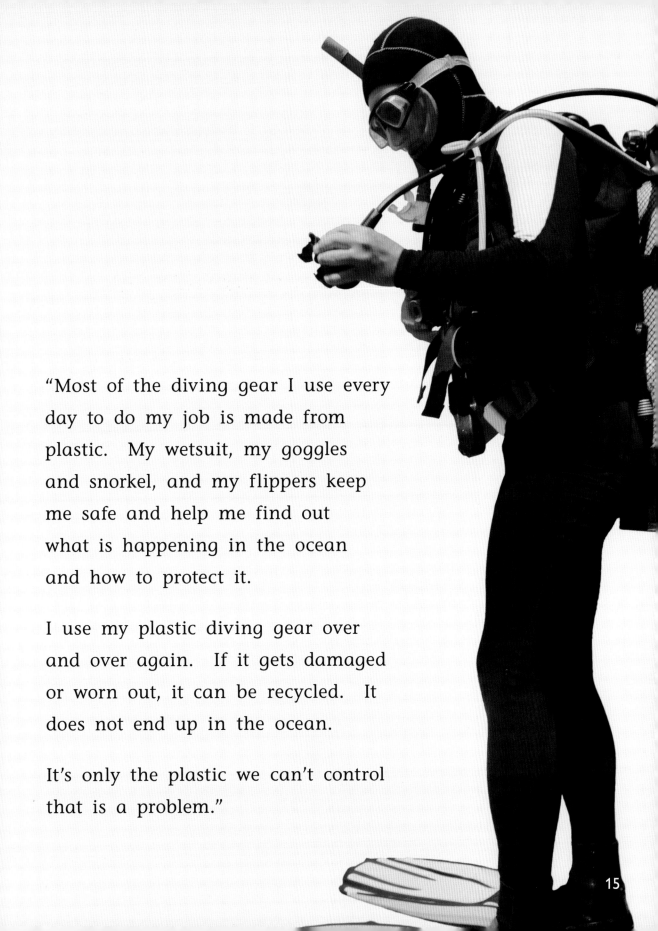

"Most of the diving gear I use every day to do my job is made from plastic. My wetsuit, my goggles and snorkel, and my flippers keep me safe and help me find out what is happening in the ocean and how to protect it.

I use my plastic diving gear over and over again. If it gets damaged or worn out, it can be recycled. It does not end up in the ocean.

It's only the plastic we can't control that is a problem."

How to write about your opinion

State your opinion

Think about the main question in the introduction on page 4 of this book. What is your opinion?

Research

Look for other information that you need to back up your opinion.

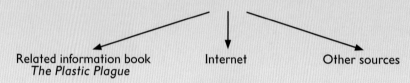

| Related information book *The Plastic Plague* | Internet | Other sources |

Make a plan

Introduction

How will you "hook" the reader to get them interested?

Write a sentence that makes your opinion clear.

List reasons to support your opinion.

| Support your reason with examples. | Support your reason with examples. | Support your reason with examples. |

Conclusion

Write a sentence that makes your opinion clear. Leave your reader with a strong message.

Publish

Publish your writing.

Include some graphics or visual images.